CONTENTS

4 WHEN WINGED CREATURES...

6 BOWEN

8 KARA

10 KING EINON

12 QUEEN AISLINN

13 FRIAR GILBERT

14 BROK

15 FELTON

16 MEET DRACO

18 DRAGONHEART - THE STORY

£5.50

WHEN WINGED CREATURES HELD DOMINION OVER THE EARTH,

Dragonheart, the smash hit movie of 1996, is a mesmerising mix of live action and stunning visual effects.

The film transports us back to a time when winged creatures ruled heaven and earth. When dragon slayers hunted dragons for bounty, forgetting that mortals once called these majestic beasts friends.

Under the rule of a bloodthirsty king, fear invaded the land. In the shadow of this tyranny, a spark of rebellion grew.

In this desperate time only one valiant Knight had the courage to overthrow the evil king and restore the glory and honour of the old code. Inspired by the ghost of King Arthur, Bowen must bring the people to victory or perish trying.

Upon the vanquished memory of Camelot's glorious promise, a murderous king builds a monument to his unrelenting greed...

BOWEN

Portrayed by Dennis Quaid.

Bowen is more noble than the king he once tutored. A courageous Knight, he turns Dragon slayer rather than betray the old code in service to a mercenary king.

Bowen's honour binds him to his vow to defend the helpless and raise his sword to defeat greed and tyranny.

Portrayed by Dina Meyer.

Like her father before her, Kara will not rest until her people are free from the tyranny of King Einon. Kara's bravery inspires Bowen to lead the battle for glory and honour.

Lee Oakes portrays young King Einon

KING EINON

Portrayed by David Thewlis.

The naive Prince who becomes a bloodthirsty King and betrays all that Bowen has taught him. Sowing starvation and misery across the land, he borrows his strength from a Dragon's heart...

AISLINN

QUEEN AISLINN

Portrayed by Julie Christie.

Queen Aislinn pleads with the Dragon to share his heart and save her only son, Einon, so that he may live to be King and uphold the Old Code, restoring peace to the land.

GILBERT

FRIAR GILBERT

Portrayed by Pete Postlethwaite. Scholar, scribe, historian and poet - Friar Gilbert boasts that he is all of these. Whilst making a pilgrimage to the lost city of Avalon, the good Friar chances upon Bowen and enrols in his cause.

BROK

Portrayed by Brian Thompson.

The villainous henchman does the sinister bidding of two kings, King Freyne and later his son, King Einon. Brok knows only the will of his sovereign.

FELTON

Portrayed by Jason Isaacs. Through his bungling, this avaricious aide to King Einon unwittingly helps the peasants in their efforts to overthrow the King.

DRACO

MEET DRACO...

MORE GLORIOUS THAN THE SUN,

MIGHTIER THAN AN ARMY.

BELIEVING IN HONOUR ABOVE ALL,

HE TRADED HIS HEART

FOR THE FREEDOM OF HUMANITY.

The commanding vocal talent of world famous actor Sean Connery brings to life the powerful personality of Draco the Dragon. The mesmerising visual effects in Dragonheart are provided by the world renowned Industrial Light & Magic Company.

DRAGONHEART: THE STORY

STEEL BLADES FLASH AND GLINT in the sun, as Sir Bowen, a fit and formidable Knight, coaches 14-year old Prince Einon in the fine art of swordplay.

"Not bad..." says Bowen, as he backwards, "...but not good enough to live."

With that, the Prince finds himself swordless, flat on his back and with the tip of Bowen's sword at his throat.

Einon kicks Bowen's blade aside, rolls over and springs up again, lunging at the Knight. Bowen deflects the blade and smiles at the boy. "That's better..."

Pleased with himself, young Einon returns the smile and relaxes his guard, just slightly, but enough for Bowen to parry and arc the flat of his sword blade down onto the youngster's shoulder. "...But you'd still be dead!"

Einon snarls angrily, then charges wildly at the Knight who laughs and leaps onto a crumbling stone wall while easily deflecting the boy's blows. "Purpose, not passion," says Bowen. "Fight with your head not your heart!"

Bowen coaches the young Prince Einon

While keeping the boy at bay, Bowen switches sword hands and pours himself a goblet of water from a flagon, a level of skill that really frustrates the Prince.

"Nerve cold-blue, blade blood-red," says Bowen, as he leaps, allowing the boy's blade to swish harmlessly beneath him. But then the wall crumbles and the Knight tumbles behind it.

"Sir Bowen?" calls the boy, scrambling over the wall to see Bowen flat on his back. As he leans down to examine him he is distracted by the sound of hoof beats. Squinting into the sun, he watches two men riding towards them. Suddenly, Bowen's sword glints at the boy's throat. "Dead again, Prince! How many times must I tell you? Only expose your back to a corpse!"

But the lesson is over and Einon greets the approaching horsemen, Lords Brok and Felton.

"The peasants are revolting," says Brok.

"They've always been revolting," replies Felton. "Smell one sometime. But now they're rebelling."

"King Freyne wants his son to witness a noble victory."

"There's nothing noble about crushing desperate, frightened men," protests Bowen.

"Traitorous scum!" says Brok. "The King commands. Bring him."

"You can watch too, nursemaid," says Felton to Bowen.

As Brok and Felton ride on, Einon turns to Bowen. "Why do you let them insult you? You, a Knight of the Old Code! You're not afraid of them."

"No," replies Bowen, "nor of their opinions. But I expect no less, they're the King's men."

Einon registers Bowen's disapproval of his father. "When I am King, you will be my man."

Bowen claps the boy's shoulder. "I am already your man, my Prince."

They ride off after Brok and Felton...

PRINCE EINON AND BOWEN arrive at a hillock overlooking a village where King Freyne presides over the destruction and carnage inflicted by his troops on the rebellious villagers below. The King spurs his charger into the heat of the battle and mows down villagers who are armed only with crude farming tools.

The rebels are driven back through their own defence lines, made from overturned carts, ditches and earthen bulwarks. Nothing stops the onslaught.

Bowen is disgusted at the sight. Einon is fascinated by it. "I wish we were down there. Just to see you in action, Bowen. Yours would be the finest blade on the field."

"Too fine to foul with your father's slaughter."

"He is my father," says Einon. "And he is the King."

Bowen accepts the admonishment. "Yes...But when you're King, remember today. Remember the difference between battle and butchery and remember the Old Code. Restore its forgotten glory, so that the crown will shine with honour once more and never again will men have to take up arms against their sovereign. Then you will be a greater King than your father."

Turning to watch the slaughter below, Bowen does not catch the dark, avaricious glint in Einon's eyes.

Suddenly, in the village below, hoards of armed peasants, led by a red-bearded rebel, burst out of hiding from huts, hayricks and houses.

Realising the danger, Freyne spurs his horse towards a bridge which is his only means of escape. But he is trapped and attacked mercilessly by the rebels.

Prince Einon sees what's happening to his father and, before Bowen can stop him, spurs his horse towards the village. Bowen gives chases while defending his young master against the angry villagers.

A band of rebels drag Freyne

Einon watches

- blood oozes from a gash over his heart.

Bowen spies Einon and spurs his steed towards him. The red-headed rebel is a girl, Kara. Even the grime of battle cannot hide her beauty. She dives out of the way as Bowen scoops up the injured boy.

"I'm here, Einon. I'm here...my King," he says, racing away with boy and crown.

IN A CASTLE at the foot of a mountain, the wounded Brok kneels before Aislinn the Queen. "Dead, Madam," he says. "King Freyne, your husband, slain."

As she takes in this news, the Queen sees Bowen silhouetted in the light of an open door with her son crumpled in his arms. "Forgive me, Queen Aislinn," says the Knight.

"It's not your fault. His father's tyranny brought him to this end."

As Bowen lays Einon gently on a bed, the boy mutters, "The crown..."

"He lives!" says the Queen.

"He dies..." says Bowen, placing the crown in Einon's hand. "He's beyond all help."

Aislinn touches a golden Dragon on the alter. "Not all..." she says, turning to the Knight.

from his saddle and set upon him with a vengeance. Soon the King's life nears its end.

"Father!" cries Einon, laying a hand on his lifeless chest...and pulling it back covered with blood.

Einon stares from his hand to the crown perched on Freyne's head. As he reaches out, Freyne's eyes flicker open. The boy hesitates a moment and then grabs the crown. The King snatches it back and for a moment father and son play a strange tug-of-war. Einon takes the crown, just as his father dies.

As Einon admires the crown, a rebel leaps on him. As they fight in a tangle of arms and legs, the rebel's bucket-like helmet falls, releasing a cascade of red hair. Einon falls on a wooden spike which pierces his chest

Freyne leads the charge on the helpless villagers

Aislinn tends to her injured son

BROK LEADS THE WAY as Aislinn and Bowen flank the palette on which Einon is being carried along a mountain path. Bowen hovers over the boy, attempting to keep him awake. "A Knight is sworn to valour," he says.

"Sworn...to...valour," mumbles the semi-conscious Einon.

"His heart knows only virtue," continues Bowen.

"...virtue..."

"His blade defends the helpless. His might upholds the weak," recites Bowen. "You must stay awake, my Lord. You must! Recite the Code..."

"...Code..."

"Yes!" says Bowen. "His might upholds the weak..."

"...His...Words speak only truth..."

"Yes...Yes..." encourages Bowen. "His wrath...?"

They recite it together, "His wrath undoes the wicked."

Eventually the party arrives at the mouth of a cave from where comes a mournful musical trilling. Queen Aislinn takes a torch and stares into the cave. Bowen lifts the young King in his arms. "This place has the stink of Dragon," he says.

"Come and fear not," says Aislinn, leading the way inside...

EVEN TORCH LIGHT cannot dispel the gloom inside the cave. Steam wreaths the place and the bones of countless creatures litter the way. Cautiously, Aislinn approaches the source of the musical trill. "Lord! Great one!" she cries.

The trilling stops. Bowen peers ahead at an uncertain shape sheathed in a glow of light.

"Your song is sad," says Aislinn.

She is answered by a sad, yet soothing voice from within the glow. "Are the stars shining tonight?" it asks.

"No bright souls glitter on this dark night," she replies.

"Aislinn, daughter of Athelstun," says the voice in recognition.

Inside the Dragon's cave

"Yes, Lord, whose people loved your kind and called them friend."

"Once. Long ago, perhaps. Now are feared...Forgotten."

"I haven't forgotten," says Aislinn. "I do not fear."

As Bowen eases Einon onto a stone plinth his eyes remain transfixed on the shape within the glow.

Aislinn kneels to comfort Einon who feverishly fondles the crown.

"Freyne's child," says the voice, "Is this why you come, Dragon slayer's wife?"

"Dragon slayer's widow," says Aislinn. "A bride of conquest! My people driven out and slaughtered the same as yours. Please...He is not his father. This Knight is his mentor. He has taught him the Old Code. And I will teach him your ways."

She unfolds Einon's undershirt, to reveal the gash above his heart.

"The wound is deep," says the voice. "You know what you ask?"

"I swear. He will grow in your grace...just and good."

"He must swear," says the voice, indicating Bowen. "Your sword, Knight."

Bowen reluctantly unsheathes his sword and hands it up.

Einon is fearful of the glow hovering above him. "Fear not," says Aislinn. "He will save you."

The shadow of a cross swings over the boy. "First, boy, swear that your father's bloodlust and tyranny die with him. Swear that you will live and rule with mercy. Come to me and learn the Once-Ways. Now swear!"

The last word echoes through the darkness.

"I...swear..." mutters Einon, raising himself up, then slumping again in Bowen's arms.

Bowen shakes the boy, "Einon? Einon! He's dead!"

In his sudden anger Bowen grabs at the sword hilt, to wrest it from the Dragon. But as he pulls it back, the Dragon's talons scrape down the length of the blade with a whining screech, scoring a groove from guard to tip.

"Peace, Knight of the Old Code," says the Dragon, his breath

Aislinn pleads with the Dragon

blowing out the torches. "Witness the wonders of an ancient glory."

Using a huge talon the Dragon lifts one of his breast scales and slices his chest, releasing a red glowing light from the wound. He leans over the boy whose face radiates as the Dragon speaks. "Half my heart to make you whole, it's strength to purify your weakness. Live and remember your oath."

A thin sliver of fire seals the boy's wound which glows with the red light of the Dragon's heart.

Bowen is astonished to see

"The wound is deep"

Einon's eyes flicker open, astonished by the miracle he has just witnessed.

More flame sprays from the Dragon, re-lighting the torches. Aislinn rises and bows to the Dragon. Bowen lifts Einon and as the entourage begins to leave the cave, he turns to the Dragon. "I've served the father only for the sake of the son. All my hopes rest on him. Forgive a doubting fool and call when you have need of me. My sword and service are yours."

The Dragon's voice answers from the gloom. "Only remind him always of his vow, Knight of the Old Code."

But, as he is transported back along the mountain trail, a strange and fierce light comes into the young King's eyes. He tries on the crown, while eyeing the ruins looming above. "The Romans built this great fortress. I will rebuild it and mine will be the greater."

Brok answers him, "It will take many men, Milord."

"Yes it will," says Einon.

LED BY BROK, Einon's soldiers swarm through the burnt out ruins of the village, rounding up the men and shackling them in wooden neck stocks. Brok orders two soldiers to pull open a cellar door and to drag out Red Beard who is hiding there.

His daughter, Kara, rushes to him, with tears in her eyes. But Brok pulls her roughly by the hair and shoves her away. Red Beard is yoked into a stock with two other prisoners.

BROK TAKES RED BEARD and the other men of the village to a quarry. Einon spots the red-haired rebel who stares at him with cold contempt.

"Come to thank me, boy?" asks Red Beard. "You should. It was my stroke that made you King."

Brok pulls Red Beard's hair and puts the dagger to his throat.

"No!" yells Einon. "I want no martyrs. And death is a release, not a punishment."

He turns to Red Beard. "Look good, dog. I'm the last thing you'll ever see." He then commands Brok to "burn the insolence out of his eyes."

As Brok picks up a red hot iron from a smithy's fire, Red Beard gazes proudly up into the rocks. Imperceptibly he shakes his head, in warning to Kara who is hiding behind a boulder.

As Brok raises the iron, Bowen's sword blade flashes down, striking it from his hand. Then the Knight gallops past Brok and slices his sword through all three wooden neck stocks. "Run!" he yells.

In the confusion the prisoners scatter into the forest. Kara scrambles out of her hiding place and rushes to her father.

Enraged, Einon draws his father's sword and makes a clumsy attack on Bowen. "How dare you defy me!"

Bowen leaps to the ground and easily knocks the sword away.

The quarry

Einon gives his orders

"Einon, you're unwell! You've been bewitched. Don't do this, remember the Code!"

"The King is above the Code," declares Einon.

"You've forgotten everything I've taught you," says Bowen sadly.

Einon attempts to fight the Knight, but Bowen easily counters each undisciplined lunge. "Purpose, not passion, Einon. Fight with your head...not your heart."

As he speaks the words, Bowen recalls with sadness that the boy's heart is now infused with the Dragon's spirit. It's almost as if he can hear the cursed heart beating, pulsing with treacherous life. With a mad, grief-stricken wail, he raises his sword...and jabs it into the ground while staring at the young King with sorrow filled eyes.

"No one is above the Code," says Bowen, his voice rasping with emotion. "Least of all the King."

With tears welling in his eyes, Bowen leans down and kisses the boy before snatching back his sword, mounting his horse and galloping away. Brok is ready to give chase.

"Let him go," says Einon. "We don't need him anymore."

Brok put the dagger to Red Beard's neck

"No one is above the Code," says Bowen. "Least of all the King."

Brok and the young King Einon

BOWEN RETURNS to the cave, but the Dragon is not there. The angry Knight clangs his sword against a rock in frustration and declares, "No matter where you fly Dragon, no matter where you hide, I'll find you. I make a new vow - I will spend the rest of my life hunting you down!"

FOURTEEN YEARS HAVE PASSED and Bowen's shield, with an awesome assortment of Dragon horns protruding from it, gives grim evidence that he has been successful in his vow. But time has been unkind to the Knight. His hair is laced with grey, his face unshaven, his surcoat frayed and torn and his armour dented and dull.

One day, as he passes by a wheat field near Felton's Mill, he comes across a frightened monk who is gathering scrolls from the ground after being unseated from his mule by a wind-whipping shadow.

"Dra...Dra...Dragon," mutters the monk.

"Where?" asks Bowen.

The Priest gestures with a bent scroll and Bowen gives chase, disappearing over the hill of wheat. Moments later the monk hears a painful howl and sees a huge explosion of dust. All goes quiet and still, then the stalks of wheat quiver as the Knight's riderless horse comes towards him...followed by Bowen, carrying a severed Dragon horn.

"Magnificent! Heroics befitting the days of Arthur and the Round Table," proclaims the monk. "Never have I seen such skill."

"Then you must have led the sheltered life of a...monk," replies Bowen.

"Also scholar, scribe, historian

and poet," says the monk. He introduces himself. "Your servant, Brother Gilbert of Glockenspur. My humble life is in the debt of your exalted prowess, dauntless courage and superb, swift sword."

"You have a poet's gift of exaggeration," observes Bowen.

"Oh Sir," says Gilbert, taking the remark as a compliment. "You should read my histories. But you belittle your talent. A great victory for you and the Lord."

"Then may the Lord savour it," says Bowen, examining the mottled, scarred horn. "There's too little glory to be shared in this kill."

"Modesty as well as valour," replies Gilbert. "The Code of Ancient Camelot still lives."

"Hardly worthy of Camelot - still, it's one less Dragon..."

Just then Lord Felton approaches, accompanied by three burly men-at-arms. "Well done, Knight," says Felton, already turning to go. "Our gratitude. Mine and King Einon's."

"Keep the gratitude," says Bowen. "I'll take gold, yours or the King's."

"Gold, Knight?"

"We struck a bargain. One Dragon put down, one pouch of gold."

Gilbert is dismayed. "Your honour has a price, Knight?"

"It has expenses. Honour cannot fill my belly or shoe my horse. I ask no more than any man. A fair price for a fair skill."

"The Priest is right," says Felton. "It's your duty to protect King Einon's vassals as a Knight of the realm."

"Not of this realm," says Bowen. "I bend no knee to Einon."

"No?" says Felton. "Then be gone, vagabond, before I arrest you for...poaching the King's wildlife."

Bowen fingers his sword hilt, debating whether to cut Felton down to size. Instead, eyeing Felton's armed guards, he smiles grimly and gives a curt bow before retrieving his horse.

As timid peasants' faces begin to poke out of the wheat, Felton turns on them. "Back to work, you lazy scum. If King Einon's wheat isn't cut before the rain, I'll do some cutting of my own."

As the men-at-arms whip the peasants back to work, Gilbert approaches Bowen. "Forgive me, Sir Knight. For questioning your motives. Times are topsy-turvy and the world is not as it once was."

"So I've noticed."

"Let me make amends. I've a fair culinary flair. Please join me in my evening repast."

"Come evening, I shall be far from here, Priest."

"So shall I," says Gilbert. "I am on a pilgrimage. Might we travel together?"

"The road is still free," says Bowen, he turns to Felton as he passes. "Unless Einon taxed it."

Felton ponders this as he watches the Knight and the monk leaving together.

Brother Gilbert of Glockenspur

Einon's hunting party

BACK AT KING EINON'S CASTLE the King's retinue are preparing for the hunt when Felton suggests the idea of a road tax. "...they use it. Let them pay for it. Those that can't, can work it off."

"Ingenious, Felton," says Einon, mounting his strong steed, then playing with a wisp of Felton's thinning hair. "There may not be much on top, but there's plenty underneath."

Felton cringes as Brok sweeps a screeching falcon close to his face. "This one loves to bring down peacocks," says Brok.

"Brok," says Einon, "some are good at hunting men. Some are good at hunting money. Both have value to me." He snatches Felton's bow and tosses it at him. "Don't forget your bow, Felton. You might cross paths with a ferocious coin purse."

Everyone laughs good-naturedly as they ride out of the castle.

THE QUARRY is now occupied by a hundred or so 'special cases' - half starved peasants who toil under the watchful eyes of the guards.

Kara, now a beautiful young woman, carries a ladle of water to her father, Red Beard, who is shaping stone with a chisel. "Drink, father."

The old man turns his blind eyes towards her. "I told you not to come here anymore."

"I am a disobedient child, Father. Drink."

His gnarled hand caresses her face. "No longer a child. A woman. And it takes no blind man to tell a beautiful one. One day one of these dogs will notice, too. Go home."

"You are my home, Father," she says, taking some cooked meat from her jerkin and stuffing it inside his shirt. "Here, for later."

As he lifts the ladle to his lips, an arrow knocks it from his hand. Kara wheels to see Einon, laughing, his bow in his hand. His hunting party follow with sleds laden with game.

"Magnificent shot, your highness," says Felton.

"Care to double the wager, Felton?"

"Alright...through his legs!"

Red Beard whirls frantically as he hears the whiz of another arrow. "Kara, what's happening?"

"Stand still, Father."

Another arrow from Einon strikes a water bucket which topples and splashes Red Beard. Kara steps bravely towards the King who aims another arrow at the girl's feet, but she keeps walking. Another arrow lands inches from her, but she keeps walking. He aims the next directly at her, but she does not flinch.

Intrigued, he lowers his bow. "You've got a nerve to interfere with the King's sport."

"There's no sport in tormenting

Red Beard implores Kara to go home

"a sick old man," says Kara. "I beg your Majesty, let him go. It's been

Kara and her father are in danger

fourteen years, your castle is built. For pity's sake, release him."

"Release him?" says Einon, as he notches another arrow and fires it straight into Red Beard's chest, the impact knocking him over. "I've always said death was a release, not a punishment."

As she runs to her dying father, Kara's wild red hair strikes some distant memory

Red Beard is struck by Einon's arrow

within the King. He spurs his horse as Red Beard dies in his daughter's arms.

Defiantly Kara watches the royal party ride away.

BESIDE A CAMPFIRE, Bowen fixes his latest Dragon's horn to his shield, while Gilbert rather overdoes his recital of a long poem about Avalon. "What do you think?" he asks.

"Avalon is a fable, Priest," answers Bowen.

"That's uneducated piffle," insists Gilbert searching for a scroll and thrusting it at Bowen. "Fact, my friend! Avalon is a holy place and my pilgrimage a sacred duty. I will find it."

"And when you do?"

"I'll pray to the souls of the sainted men buried there. King Arthur and all the Knights of The Round Table. I'll pray for a return of the Old Code, for a society of brotherhood and justice."

"The Old Code? No prayers can resurrect that pale ghost," reflects Bowen.

"Ride with me, my son. All Knights need a quest. I think ours is the same."

"Men of faith may follow a fable, Priest. But my only faith is my sword. And I already have a quest."

"What quest?"

"To slay all Dragons. And one in particular..."

Gilbert's face lights up in awe and pleasure - he's found the hero of his next epic poem!

DRAGON TRACKS mark the sandy bank of a shallow creek. Bowen

Friar Gilbert sits on a 'rock'

jerks up his lance and reins his horse towards a nearby waterfall, his Dragon will be there.

"Yoo-hoo!" calls Gilbert, standing atop a rock on the opposite bank.

Bowen rides over to him, muttering. "What are you doing here?"

"How do you prefer I write this?" asks Gilbert, pulling out ink and parchment.

"Far away!"

But Gilbert doesn't get it. "Please, don't concern yourself with my safety. I meant style...verse... metre. Shall I spice it up with a poetical flourish or just the cold hard facts?"

"Ssssh!" says Bowen, poking his lance through the scroll and jerking it away. "We'll be the only things cold and hard around here if you don't shut up!"

"That's a fine attitude," says Gilbert, indignantly keeping pace with the Knight along the rocks near the waterfall. "I come to immortalise you and you try to muzzle the mouth of chronicle, lop off the tongue of truth. It's all very well to go about hacking and whacking Dragons..."

He sits on a rock and scribbles away with a sharp quill, not noticing a giant eye opening up beneath him. The 'rock' shivers and twitches as he continues. "...You're nothing without the likes of me. Heroics don't make heroes, ballad-makers do. The quill is mightier than the swo..." The 'rock' shivers again, then starts to shudder and rise. "...ord...duh...duh ...ahh!"

The monk tumbles off and splashes into the water beside Bowen.

The Knight whirls at the sound of more splashing, just in time to see a Dragon's tail slither along the creek and disappear into the waterfall. The 'rock' on which Gilbert was perched has also gone.

Bowen spurs his horse towards the cave, but is halted by a flying breastplate. "That's all that's left of the last fellow who entered here uninvited," calls the Dragon from within the waterfall.

"Doesn't frighten me," says Bowen.

"No? How about this? Or this? Or this?" A barrage of crumpled armour and bones careens out, followed by the complete skeleton of a horse and rider. The splash washes over Gilbert and sends him flopping into the stream. He shrieks as a helmeted head lands in his lap!

"I could go on," says the Dragon. "I have quite a collection."

"I won't add to it," replies Bowen, as he charges into the waterfall.

Suddenly his lance is yanked so severely that he spills from the saddle and somersaults into the water. Moments later the two halves of his broken lance shoot out of the cave.

As Bowen draws his sword and shield and walks into the cave, a flash of flame lights up the waterfall and a blast of steam rolls out.

Bowen's sword rises into a bright beam of light

INSIDE THE DRAGON'S CAVE, flames deflect against Bowen's shield. Sparks hiss and smoke against the damp floor. The Knight grins up at the Dragon lurking on a shelf of rock in the darkness above him. "Little damp for a fire, isn't it?"

"Why must you Knights always pick on us Dragons?"

"It's honest enough work, ridding the country of you lot. One must earn a living."

"Yes, one must live," says the Dragon. "Well, since you seek a profit, we might as well begin."

"Don't flatter yourself. It's not the profit, it's the pleasure..."

As Bowen's sword rises into a bright beam of light, the Dragon's eyes widen as he recognises the talon-scratched groove in the blade. "Perhaps less pleasurable and more costly than you think," he says before, swooping down off the ledge and out of the waterfall.

His magnificent wings are spread to their full width. He is an awesome, glorious creature. Patches of his hide glisten iridescently as he sweeps over the startled Gilbert before rising higher and higher into the sky.

Bowen dashes out of the cave, climbs onto his horse and gallops into the woods after the Dragon who is now skimming the treetops.

Riding at full speed Bowen puts the reins in his teeth and yanks a set of knotted strings from his saddle bags which open to reveal a chain-spindle and a catapult. He reaches a clearing then fires, catapulting three bolo balls skywards. They spread and spin in the air and snare the Dragon's hind leg.

The Dragon is ensnared

Bowen quickly wraps the chain around his saddle cleat, but the power of the Dragon snaps the clinches and the Knight, still in his saddle, slides off the horse. He clutches the chain for dear life and is dragged along, bouncing through the undergrowth. The Dragon swings him towards a huge tree and just before impact, Bowen jumps off the saddle and wedges it in a fork of the tree. He drops down as timber crashes all around

The Dragon's tail wedges in a log

him. He rolls free in time to see the snared Dragon crash behind the

Bowen takes a swing at the Dragon's tail

ridge line.
   Bowen finds the Dragon in a clearing, struggling to untangle the snare from his leg. "Fleeing from an honourable challenge? What kind of Dragon are you?"
   "You won't live long enough to find out, dear boy," says the Dragon, swiping at the Knight with his tail.
   Bowen blocks the blow with his blade, but is almost unbalanced. The tail smashes against his shield, knocking him back into a tree. He ducks just in time to avoid another blow. The tail misses him and slices the tree in half.
   "You're good," says Bowen. "Haven't had this sort of challenge in some time."
   "Nor likely to again," responds the Dragon, flailing once more, missing the Knight and wedging his tail like an axe in a fallen tree. He tugs, trying to pull the tail out, bouncing the tree up and down.
   With the tail stuck, Bowen takes his chance and cautiously approaches the Dragon. "Over-confident, aren't we?"
   "Hardly," says the Dragon, manoeuvring to confront the Knight. "But if you win, you'll be out of work."
   "Ha! I'll keep on till I've exterminated every last one of you."
   "I am the last one."
   This stops Bowen in his tracks.

He drops his guard...as the Dragon snorts a fireball from his nostril. The Knight leaps back behind a rock as a second fireball flies towards him. "You're just trying to save your scaly hide with tricks."
   "Haven't you noticed the pickings are rather slim these days?" asks the Dragon.

Stalemate!

"I got one just the other day," says Bowen, tapping the latest addition on his Dragon-horned shield.

"So, you killed the Scarred One. He and I were the last. Must have been a proud kill warrior. How much gold did his tattered carcass put in your purse?"

"That's none of your business," says Bowen, stepping closer to the bolo rope still wrapped around the Dragon's leg.

"Couldn't have been much," says the Dragon. "When there are no more Dragons to slay, how will you make a living?"

"Shut up," says Bowen, straddling the rope while raising his sword to strike.

The Dragon jerks his foot, the rope snaps up and sends Bowen flying, losing his shield in the process. The animal rears up, his jaw distending like a snake's, stretching wider as sharp fangs suddenly spring out.

Gilbert screeches and covers his eyes.

Bowen lays in the darkness inside the jaws, his sword-tip tickling the Dragon's palette. "If your teeth come down, my sword goes up. Right into your brain..."

A SILVER MOON LIGHTS THE GLADE. Dragon and Knight remain in the same positions. Gilbert, wearily watching the scene, flops asleep on his parchment.

The Dragon's jaw is stretched to its aching maximum. "Ibf your sworb cums up, ma teef cum down," he mumbles.

Bowen crouches uncomfortably inside the huge mouth, propping his sword arm up with his other hand. He spies a piece of cloth stuck between the back teeth and gives it a tug. It is a sleeve, with a skeletal hand still inside. He recognises the ring on the bony finger. "Good Lord, Sir Eglamore." He drops the hand.

"Thanffs!" says the Dragon. "Been stug upf dere fa monffs. Cuud you ged your elba aff ma tongue?"

"Why should you be comfortable? My armour is rusting in your drool," says Bowen. "And your breath is absolutely foul!"

The Dragon starts to cough and a huge ball of saliva rolls up his throat and smacks Bowen in the face.

"Hey! Watch it!"

"Sorry," says the Dragon. "Id seems we'rr in a bid ab a stalemade, wuudn't you thay?"

"I can go three days without sleep," says Bowen.

"I can go fhree weegs."

"I'll stab you before I nod off."

The Dragon is peeved. "Und I'll chompf you. We'd kull eagh ofper."

"What do you suggest?"

"A troose! Ged out aff ma mouf and led's tag face-ta-face."

"How do I know I can trust you?"

"I gib you ma word."

"A Dragon's word is worthless."

"Stubborn lout," says the Dragon, arching his tongue and causing Bowen to slide off his slippery perch, his sword clattering to the ground.

The Dragon clamps him down with a scaly claw, his eyes searing into him as he shakes his jaws back in place.

Bowen is clamped by the Dragon's scaly claw

The Dragon flies, the peasants flee

"I should have known," says Bowen. "Go on, kill me."

"I don't want to kill you," says the Dragon. "I never did! And I don't want you to kill me. How do we gain? If you win, you lose your trade. If I win, I wait around for the next sword slinger thirsting to carve a reputation out of my hide. I'm tired of lurking in holes and skulking in darkness. I'm going to let you get up now and if you insist, we can pursue this fracas to its final stupidity. Or you can listen to my alternative."

The Dragon releases Bowen and drops to the ground, exhausted. Bowen drops too. "What alternative?"

NEXT MORNING, still laying on his epic poem, Gilbert snorts, stirs and rises. Suddenly remembering the night before, he staggers to his feet in a panic. He looks around, but sees nothing except smouldering wood, and the bony hand of Sir Eglamore in a bush. He picks it up, believing it to be Bowen's hand. "Poor chap. Picked clean."

He crosses himself and sadly crumples the ink-blotched parchment in his hands.

WORKERS AT FELTON'S MILL, are terrified to see the Dragon flying overhead. They run from the wheat field as he unleashes two streams of flame from his nostrils. He sweeps through the column of smoke and wings his way to the mill, shooting two more fire balls. The first blows the roof off the storehouse, the second blasts two tons of flour into the air.

As Felton surveys the confusion, Bowen, armed to the teeth, rides up behind him. "Pesky critters, Dragons," he says. "Like big rodents. You never seem to get rid of them..."

BOWEN NEGOTIATES to rid Felton of the Dragon. The fee, paid in advance, even includes the money Felton withheld the last time.

With the help of the workers Bowen constructs a huge catapult, called a 'Whacker' and loads it with a heavy harpoon, just in time to see the Dragon skimming towards them across the lake. Bowen takes aim, slices the rope-trigger with his sword, and the harpoon flies towards its target.

In mid-flight, the Dragon skilfully catches the harpoon under his wing and clamps his claw on the shaft, while letting out a loud moan.

To Felton's crowd it appears that Bowen has scored a direct hit, especially when the Dragon acts out a spectacular 'death scene', pirouetting in the air before slipping beneath the lake's surface with hardly a splash.

With the Dragon submerged, Felton turns to his thugs. "Get my money back," he orders.

Bowen whistles his horse and leaps into the saddle as it gallops past. He rides off, weighing the money pouch in his hands. The thugs are too far back to be a threat.

THE DRAGON SWIMS GRACEFULLY beneath the crystal surface of the lake, before surfacing near a bank where a flock of sheep are grazing. His eyes gleam and his tongue flicks hungrily across his lips. "Hellooo..." he says.

AS BOWEN RIDES ALONG, counting the day's takings, the Dragon floats belly-up beside him in the air.

"Most profitable," says Bowen. "I should have met you long ago."

"There is much gold in the world. When you have your fill of it and no longer need me..."

"I am a Knight of the Old Code. My word is my bond."

The Dragon floats around Bowen. "No compunctions then?"

"About what?"

"Well," says the Dragon, a puff of fleece shooting from his mouth, "such a deception hardly befits a Knight of the Old Code."

"Fleecing Einon's lackeys is a service to mankind."

"Is it?" asks the Dragon, puffing out more fleece. "When you squeeze the nobility, it's the peasants who feel the pinch."

"Why should I stick my neck out for people afraid to risk their own? If I wanted my conscience pricked, I'd have stayed with the Priest. What does a Dragon know of the Old Code anyway?"

The Dragon quotes, "'His blade defends the helpless. His might upholds the weak...His words speak only truth.'"

"Shut up! I remember," snaps Bowen. "And that's all it is - a memory. Nothing...nothing can bring it back."

"You sound like one who tried..."

"And failed," says Bowen. "I no longer try to change the world, Dragon. I just try to get by in it."

"Yes...It's better than death, I suppose."

"Oh, is it?...I should think you'd welcome death. You know, the last of your race. All your friends dead. Hated and hunted wherever you go..."

"Do you delight in reminding me," answers the Dragon, coldly. "Yes, I do long for death...but fear it."

"Why? Aside from your misery, what's to lose."

"My soul."

Bowen takes this in, then rides away. The Dragon lumbers after him.

RAUCOUS LAUGHTER ECHOES from within the towering walls of Einon's castle, as the King, his Knights and their womenfolk dine by torch light.

Atop the table, Brok wrestles two men at once. He flings one over his shoulder and into the bonfire, much to the approval of the lords and ladies. As Brok tightens a hammer lock on his other opponent's head, a coarse woman leaps onto her chair yelling, "Twist it off, lovey," before grabbing Brok by the hair and planting a big, sloppy kiss on him.

Brok slings the wrestler down the length of the table, sending food and crockery flying. He slides to the end where he groans and passes out, with his head almost in Queen Aislinn's lap.

"Can he continue Mother?" asks Einon.

In dainty disgust, Aislinn lifts the unconscious man's arm off her

plate and drops it contemptuously

Einon presides over dinner

over the edge of the table. "The field is Sir Brok's, my son."

The King turns to Felton. "That's twenty you owe me," he says scooping two stacks of coins into his arms.

Felton tries to protest.

"Ten...my son," corrects Aislinn.

But Felton slides the two piles back to Einon. "The spectacle of Sir Brok's prowess is worth double the wager, sire! That and his lovely wife's devotion."

As Einon snatches up a pitcher of wine he sees, reflected in the polished sheen of the metal, a figure armed with a knife, creeping down the low rooftop directly behind him.

Suddenly the figure leaps at him. But Einon's timing is perfect - he turns and slams the intruder onto the table, amidst the screams of the shocked women. He is on top of the body in an instant, spinning it around and wrenching the knife away.

It is Kara! With her red hair flying wildly she struggles in Einon's grasp as half-a-dozen swords are drawn, ready to end her life.

"No!" cries Einon, scrutinising the girl. "I know you...The quarry! The blind dog's whelp! Family

devotion is a fine thing. Isn't it, Mother?"

Sad Aislinn, her eyes filled with quiet admiration for the girl, refuses to answer the sneering question.

Einon turns on Kara. "First you beg for mercy for your father's fate. Then try to avenge it. Now you'll share it."

"In your kingdom, Einon, there are worse fates than death," says Kara.

"I'll think one up for you. Lock her up."

Felton and others haul Kara

Felton hauls Kara away

away.

Einon picks up the dagger and gazes at his mother. She watches him in inscrutable silence.

EINON BARGES INTO THE DUNGEON, startling Kara who is chained to the wall.

"I remember now...your hair...like fire...you gave me this wound," he says, opening his shirt to reveal his thick, ugly knotted scar. "I owe you," he says, sliding the carved handle of the dagger across her cheek and throat. "I remember everything now. Everything..."

LATER, TEARS GLISTEN in Kara's eyes. "You weep?" says Einon. "You could be on the battlements as buzzard bait rather than in the royal bed. Rebels must learn to love their King."

As Einon weaves to the night stand to refill his wine cup, Kara spies his discarded belt on the floor, with her dagger tucked inside it...

Bowen and the Dragon talk about Einon

BOWEN AND THE DRAGON camp on a plateau. A skinned rabbit is skewered on a spit as the Knight attempts to light a fire. Suddenly flames snort out of the Dragon's

The Dragon lights the campfire

nostrils, burning the campfire and the rabbit. "Hope you like it well done!" he says, wiping black rings from his snout.

Later, as Bowen sharpens his sword with a whetstone, he accidentally kicks over his shield, ringed with Dragon horns.

"You must have hated us very much," says the Dragon.

"I hated one of you. But I never found him. I never will. If you're the last, he must be dead."

"Tell me what he was like?"

"He only had half a heart. But even that was enough to pollute an innocent."

The Dragon rises up, hotly. "Einon was no innocent! He polluted the heart!"

Now Bowen rises. "How do you know that, Dragon?"

The Dragon becomes evasive. "Well, all dragons know it. What was to be their hope became their doom. A spoiled, ungrateful child was given a great gift and destroyed it!"

"No!" says Bowen. "I knew Einon. I was his teacher. I taught him the ways of honour and right."

"Then he betrayed you, Bowen, just as he betrayed the Dragon whose heart he broke."

As Bowen feeds more wood into the dwindling fire, the Dragon falls, wincing, to the ground...a red glow pulsates beneath the skin of his ailing left shoulder...

...EINON SLUMPS AGAINST THE WALL of his bedchamber, with Kara's dagger buried in his left shoulder. "A love dart, from Cupid," she glares.

But the King wrenches the blade free and exposes only a thin trickle of blood. He laughs, wiping the blood and sucking it from his finger. "Not as deep or deadly as you thought? Next time stab more flesh, less cloth."

"Next time I'll pierce your heart," says Kara.

"You already did, sweet, in more ways than one," he says, placing her hand against his chest. "A very special heart like no other."

"A black, withered thing without pity," says Kara.

A pathetic look of pain enters Einon's eyes as his hand entwines in her hair. "Then teach me. Pity me...I would give you everything. Even power. You are so beautiful." He kisses her reluctant lips. "Even power...even a throne..."

As Einon staggers drunkenly from the room, Kara fights back fresh tears. Her hands scrape down her body as though trying to rub his foul touch from her.

STEAM SIZZLES AND HISSES through the wet saddle blanket laid across the Dragon's shoulder. "Oh dear. Thank you. It's passed now," he says to Bowen.

"What was it?"

"An old complaint that acts up now and again..."

"Forgive me if I upset you."

"It wasn't you...not you."

AS KARA STARES OUT OF THE WINDOW HOLES, longing for escape, a shadow falls over her. "How did you get in here?" she asks, as Aislinn steps into the firelight.

"I have my ways. I've come to help."

"I need no help from the beast's mother."

"I was the mother of an innocent child. It wasn't his fault, he was the fruit of a seed sown without love."

"I would have smothered him in his crib," says Kara.

"You think so now," says the Queen. "I thought so once. But when you hold a child in your arms

you don't see the monster he could become...Only a small something that is part of you, crying for your nourishment, frail and helpless. Then suddenly you realise it's you,

Kara longs to escape

you are the one that's helpless. I could not guide him. I was merely a prize of conquest...allowed no pleasure, no feelings. No chance to be his mother. There was nothing left for him but his father's taint."

"Is this the help you offer?" asks Kara. "To foretell my future in your past? Then give me the dagger. Let me kill myself."

"Do not wish for death, girl, when there's freedom," says Aislinn, pressing a hidden spring in a corner of the room. As she does so, a huge hearth slides back to reveal a secret passage.

The Queen leads Kara along a stone path, then points to stairs leading to an iron door. Kara turns to thank her, but Aislinn has disappeared into the shadows.

ON LEARNING OF KARA'S ESCAPE, Einon flies into a rage. He flings one guard across the room and another into the open fireplace. "Dogs! Fools! If you can't guard a simple girl, then go guard shadows in hell!"

Brok intervenes. "Sire! There's no way she could've slipped past them."

Einon spins on Brok, brandishing the tip of a poker against his throat. "What are you saying?"

"There are only two ways out of here," explains Brok. "And only one is obvious."

"Yes," says Einon, his gaze shifting to his mother. "How could the girl have known?" He orders Brok to send his best men to find Kara.

"I'll send someone to clean up this mess," says Aislinn, coolly.

Einon watches her suspiciously as she leaves.

"I'VE BEEN THINKING," says Bowen as he watches over the wounded Dragon on the plateau.

"About what?"

"Mostly what to call you. I've found you a name."

"You say that as if you reached up and plucked it out of the sky."

"I did," replies Bowen, looking up. "See that cluster of stars there."

"I know those stars very well."

"Do you see the shape they make?"

The Dragon gazes up, then back at Bowen. "Mm-hmm, a Dragon."

"Yes. We call it Draco. It means 'dragon' in the scholar's speech."

"I would be honoured to be named after those stars. Thank you."

KARA IS PELTED WITH FRUIT AND VEGETABLES as she tries to stir the villagers to rebellion.

"Throw off the yoke of Einon's oppression," she cries. "We work hard and he takes it all to feed his dreams of conquest."

Another rotten cabbage ploughs into her chest and a glob of mud smacks her forehead.

"...Listen to me! He's made you slaves! It's time to fight back!"

"Your father sang that sour song once, and we did fight back," yells One-Eyed Hewe the blacksmith, pointing to his eye patch. "Once was enough. We'll not dance to it again."

"No, just cringe like dogs under Einon's boot," says Kara.

"A cringing dog's a live one!" says Hewe. He is about to throw a squash when it is grabbed from his hand by Bowen.

Kara smiles at the Knight in recognition.

"Why waste good food on bad rhetoric?" asks Bowen, biting into the squash.

"I speak the truth," says Kara, the smile disappearing from her face.

"Truth is rarely inspiring, lass, and it never wins rebellions. But it can stretch rebel's necks...If there is a neck under that vegetable patch."

Self-consciously, Kara wipes her face as Bowen offers her the other half of the squash. She shoves it into his face and the crowd laugh.

Just then an old crone screams and points skywards in speechless horror as Draco swoops over the village,

"About time," mutters Bowen, as the Dragon knocks a patch of thatch from a roof. "Show off..."

Bowen bargains with Hewe to rid the village of the Dragon, who is now perched on a rocky ledge and putting on an awesome display of fire spray. "Where's the Lord responsible for this village?" Bowen asks.

"Brok lives in a fine house six miles away. He'll just blame any destruction on us and pluck our pockets to pay for it."

"Well, I won't pluck them as deeply. It's a fair offer. Take it or leave...him," says Bowen, pointing to Draco.

Kara shoves her way through. "It's bad enough you grovel to Einon," she says to the villagers. "Will you now be bullied by some blackmailing, broken-down

One-Eyed Hewe

Knight?"

Bowen glares at her, then turns to a rotund villager standing with his three rotund daughters. "Perhaps you'll part with one of your delectable daughters instead of gold. Dragons are partial to maiden sacrifices I hear!"

The man put a protective arm in front of his daughters. But Hewe has another idea. "Why must it be

Draco gives an awesome display of fire spray

a daughter?" he asks, turning his gaze on Kara, whose jaw drop in disbelief.

Draco watches the villagers, as they wheel Kara, strapped on a wooden cart, towards an open field. "Who's the girl?" he asks Bowen.

"A nuisance. Get rid of her...They're trying to placate you with a sacrifice."

"Whoever gave them that bright idea?"

"Never mind. They're imbeciles...Just get rid of her."

"How?"

"Eat her!"

"Oh, please," says Draco. "Yecch!"

"My, aren't we squeamish. You ate Sir Eglamore."

"I merely chewed in self defence! I never swallowed."

"Well...then...improvise..." says Bowen, as Draco swoops off the rock towards Kara, who screams and faints when he reaches out a claw to her. He wrenches the limp girl off the cart and carries her away...

KARA SITS ON A ROCK beside a waterfall. She is enchanted by the strange trilling of Draco's dragonsong. "You have a beautiful voice."

"We Dragons love to sing when we're happy."

"You're not like a Dragon at all," she says.

"How many Dragons do you know?" asks Draco, oozing charm and sidling up to her.

"Well, none. But you're supposed to eat people, not serenade them. You don't seem to do any of the terrible things people say you do."

"Nah, that's minstrel's fancies. I never hurt a soul unless they try to hurt me first."

"Then why were you in my village?" asks Kara.

"Oh?...Oh!...The village!

Kara is enchanted by Draco's dragonsong

"Yes!" says Bowen, charging up the stream, "you remember the village."

Misunderstanding his intentions, Kara lets out a warlike screech, leaps onto Bowen's horse and begins to pummel him. "Leave him alone you bully," she cries. "Run, Draco. Fly! I'll hold him."

They tumble into the stream. Bowen gets to his feet and turns to Draco. "Where have you been?"

"I've been distracted," says Draco. "Bowen, meet Kara."

Bowen grabs the girl's floundering arm to help her up, but she slaps him away and flops back into the water.

"You should have eaten her," says Bowen.

Suddenly Einon, Brok and their search party emerge from the trees. Bowen leaps protectively in front of Kara, his sword whirling and flashing.

Einon laughs as he recognises Bowen. "It can't be! But it is! The King's old mentor still giving carving lessons."

"Get off your horse and I'll give you one."

"I'm bigger now," says the King. "Perhaps I'll give you one."

"Stick to slaughtering peasants. It's safer."

"We don't slaughter them anymore, they can't pay their taxes if they're dead," says Einon, surveying Bowen's ragged condition. "Seems times have not been kind. You should never have broken with me."

"It was you who broke with me," replies Bowen with a twisted smile.

"Yet you return to me," says the King. "And with my lost lady."

Bowen turns to Kara who shakes her head in vigorous denial. "I think the lady wants to stay lost."

"Not her choice, I'm afraid," says Einon.

Kara and Draco

"My three feet of steel says it is."

Angered, Einon draws his sword. "I'm ready for my lesson now, Knight..."

He flings his shield at Bowen, who dodges it and deftly rolls to protect himself as the King charges over to Kara and grabs her by the hair. "Don't go anywhere, sweet. This won't take long," he says, kissing her ruthlessly.

Bowen springs up and slams the shield against Einon's back, unseating him from his horse. "Only expose your back to a corpse. That's one lesson you never learned."

Einon's men start to rush in, but he orders them to stand off and turns to Bowen, "You are a corpse. You just don't know it."

They trade fast and furious blows, as Draco watches from behind the waterfall. The swordplay is dazzling - but Einon is younger and faster. "Lie down, Bowen," he says. "Life has passed you by. You're the sorry scrap of a dead world and dead beliefs."

Bowen gasps angrily. "They were your beliefs. You spoke the words! You spoke them from your heart."

"I vomited them because I couldn't stomach them," spits Einon. "I knew it was what you wanted to hear."

"Lies," says Bowen. "I taught you..."

"...to fight! That's all. I took what I needed from you Knight. You taught me to fight. You taught me well!"

Bowen's dreams are shattered. He attacks sloppily and the young King's blade rips across his shoulder, sending the disillusioned Knight spinning back onto his knees.

Before Einon can deliver the death blow, Draco swoops in, landing between the two men. His wings open and the scales on his chest fall back exposing the red scar on his chest. The King reels in fearful recognition, dashes to his horse and gallops away.

Bowen staggers out of the water. "Who asked you to butt in? I had everything under control."

Draco does not answer. Disturbed, he watches Einon riding away.

Bowen and Einon fight by the waterfall

Draco, Bowen and Kara

KARA WALKS BESIDE BOWEN as he leads his horse over a river near a marshland village. He winces, rubbing his wounded shoulder.

"Here, let me see," says Kara, opening his jerkin and tenderly removing the ragged bandage. She looks up and catches him staring at her, but he turns away. "It's almost healed. Another few days and it'll be just another scar."

"It's knitted tight," agrees Bowen. "Next village ought to give it a little exercise."

"But no medicine for your other wound," says Kara.

"I have no other wound."

"But I do. It hurts to find your heroes are just charlatans looking out for themselves."

"That's the way the wretched world turns, girl."

"And what about those who can't look out for themselves?" she asks. "You could lead them, Bowen. You could give them courage and hope."

"False hope," replies Bowen. "Even if you could raise a ragtag army, what chance would they have against seasoned troops? The last time they tried, it ended up a massacre. I remember! I was there!"

"So was I," says Kara. "And I remember more. I remember one lone Knight who dared to stand against the King and saved a rebel leader from being blinded..."

Bowen turns sharply, as Kara continues, "...for a little while anyway. That was you Bowen. The rebel was my father."

Bowen looks at her, the memory slowly crystallising.

"Let others stand with you," she says, "and this time the end will be different."

He takes her gently by the shoulders and gazes sadly into her beautiful angry eyes.

"What are you looking at?" she asks.

"Myself once upon a time..."

Draco's shadow passes overhead.

"I'll see you in the village, Draco," says Bowen riding away.

"What will you do, Kara?" asks Draco.

"Try to turn the wretched world the other way," she answers. "Einon must be brought down."

"Einon will not fall in my lifetime," says Draco, swooping off down river.

BOWEN SWATS AWAY MOSQUITOES as he rides into the marshland village where some huts are ablaze, the result of a 'dragon attack'.

The Knight is soon bargaining with the villagers to rid them of the Dragon and the village chief hands him a money sack. But suddenly Kara arrives, pushing through the press of villagers. "Wait!" she says, "This man is a fraud!"

As the chief jerks the money back, Bowen thrusts out his dragon-horn shield. "This is no fraud. That girl's a wandering idiot, babbling nonsense!"

"I'm telling you, this Knight is no dragon slayer," says Kara.

Just then Friar Gilbert arrives on the scene, his parchment sack slung over his back. "You're mistaken, my child."

"Brother Gilbert!" cries Bowen.

"Bowen my lad. Praise the Saints, you're alive...and whole!" says Gilbert, turning to the Chief. "You couldn't put your trust in a better man. I have personally seen him slay almost two dragons."

"Almost?" asks Kara.

"Well I didn't actually witness the deathblow to the second. But since Sir Bowen's here, he must have won!"

That convinces the Chief. He hands the money back to Bowen.

"No!" yells Kara. "Don't you understand. He's in league with the Dragon!"

Everyone laughs as Bowen makes a 'crazy' sign at Kara.

Bowen, Kara and Gilbert attempt to flee from the angry villages

HELPED BY GILBERT, BOWEN HAS constructed another 'Whacker' catapult. Kara watches him. "I thought you had sunk low, Bowen. But not this low!"

"Wait till you see how low Draco sinks," answers Bowen.

Sure enough, Draco wings downstream on another 'raid'. Bowen slices the rope-trigger and the harpoon flies at Draco who expertly snares the lance beneath his wing, before going into his 'death throes' and plunging into the marsh. But this time, instead of a graceful entry into the water, there is a horrible muck exploding impact as the Dragon lands belly-up in five feet of water, frozen in an awkward death pose.

"Well, sink...sink!" whispers Bowen.

"I can't," mutters the Dragon. "It doesn't get any deeper."

Gilbert runs up. "You've done it again, Sir Knight," he says, joyously. "Look at the brute, even bigger than the last one."

"Actually, he's about the same size," says Bowen.

Just then a band of villagers, yelling "Meat! Meat! Meat!" charge at the two tons of free food laying in the marsh.

"Uh-oh," says Bowen, as Draco breaks his death pose and jerks his head up.

"Good Lord, he's alive!" exclaims Gilbert.

"Get it while it's still down," yells the Chief.

Just as the villagers get within striking distance, Draco flips over, starts running then whooshes off the water and into the air.

The villagers turn angrily on Bowen, chanting "Meat! Meat! Meat!" again.

Bowen leaps onto his horse, scoops Kara up and charges through the mob.

Gilbert is utterly baffled, he turns but runs straight into the Chief who raises a huge cleaver above him. Before it comes down on the Priest, Bowen slings the money sack at the Chief, yelling, "Satisfaction guaranteed or your money back."

He heaves Gilbert onto the horse but, whichever way they turn, they are surrounded by angry villagers. It looks bad, until Draco swoops down and scoops up the horse and its three riders - leaving the villagers astonished.

"SAINTS PRESERVE US," yells Gilbert, as Draco banks into a thick layer of low-ceilinged cloud. "I nearly have my bald pate trimmed at the neck. Bowen, I find you in league with a dragon who kidnaps me...and now we're lost in this dreadful fog!"

The mysterious castle

"Not lost. Never lost," says Draco.

Up ahead the ruins of a once magnificent ancient castle loom out of the thinning mist. "What deadly, unholy place is this?" asks Gilbert.

"More than death lives here, Brother," says Draco.

"Wh-what more?"

"A spirit. Beyond death...alive and eternal...that remembers the Once-Ways and the glory of one who shared our name."

"What one?"

"The Pendragon!"

"Pend...Arthur Pendragon? King Arthur! A land of mist...Avalon! Bowen, we've found Avalon!" exclaims Gilbert as Draco drifts over the fortress walls.

GILBERT PRAYS BEFORE THE TALLEST COLUMN in a circle of stones. "So it was foretold. And, O, I have found you brave King Arthur. Among your brother Knights in a grove upon a tor...The Round Table of Camelot..."

Bowen moves solemnly among the columns, talking to himself, touching the stones. "...Here was Sir Gawain's place...Here Galahad..."

Gilbert continues his prayer. "Let us who remember the glories of your Golden Kingdom feel your noble Spirit, O King..."

Bowen weaves through the columns. "Lancelot...the right hand of King Arthur..."

Gilbert continues. "...and let the song of Excalibur echo in our enemy's ear as we set out to strike down tyranny once and for all...Amen..."

As Gilbert rises, he turns to Bowen. "My son, this is Avalon, the shadow realm of the Round Table. It is a divine omen."

"Omens and shadows won't

Draco tells Bowen a tale of long ago

Draco and Bowen look up to the stars

win battles," replies Bowen. "Nor will you. You'll know disappointment when you try to raise your 'army'."

He turns to Kara, "You already know the courage of your village. They're very brave at pelting girls with vegetables."

"It must start somewhere," says Kara. She looks up at Draco perched on a crumbling turret and gazing at the star-filled sky. "We wish you luck."

"Long ago," says Draco, "when man was young and the Dragon already old, the wisest of our race took pity on man and shared with him our secrets. When this wise one was dying, he gathered together all the Dragons, making them vow to watch over man always. And at the moment of his death the night became alive with all those stars."

He looks up at the glittering Draco constellation. "Through the years, his shimmering soul was joined by others, as the Dragons kept their pledge to serve man...until the heavens were aglow with stars."

He looks down again at the trio below. "But then man grew arrogant with the gift of our power and shunned our guidance and no

The proud Draco

more stars ascended the sky to hold back the darkness. All my life I've longed to perform one deed worthy of those forever shining above. Finally my chance came. A great sacrifice that would reunite man and Dragon and ensure my place among my ancient brothers in the sky...But my sacrifice became my sin."

In that moment realisation comes to Bowen. "It was you. Your half-heart beats in Einon's breast."

Draco descends into the circle to

face his friend. "Yes. My half-heart that cost me all my soul. Even then I knew his bloodthirsty nature, but I thought my heart could change him. My God, I was naive."

"No more than I," admits Bowen. "Always I dreamed of serving noble Kings and nobler ideals. But dreams die hard and you hold them in your hands long after they've crumbled to dust. I will not be that naive again."

"Kara," says Draco, "I will go with you."

Bowen, stunned by Draco's declaration, turns and walks out of the circle.

"So be it," says Draco. "Farewell, Bowen."

ALONE, BOWEN SHELTERS in the hollow of a crumbling turret. Pulling his cloak about him to keep out the wind-whipped chill, he hears a ghostly whisper. "Valour...Valour..."

He springs up, peering into rainy, windswept mist. The whisper comes again, "Valour."

Bowen whirls to the voice, coming from the stone columns. "A Knight is sworn to valour..."

Another voice joins in, "His heart knows only virtue..."

Bowen walks from his shelter, listening as a third voice joins in...then a fourth, "His blade defends the helpless"... "His might upholds the weak..."

The hollow voices echo and overlap in the wind. Then Lancelot's voice floats out of his stone, "His words speak only truth..."

Then, majestic and eternal, King Arthur emerges from his stone, fifteen feet high, bursting with power and shedding golden light. Bowen collapses to his knees as Arthur speaks. "His wrath undoes

Bowen is left alone

the wicked."

More ghostly voices of the Round Table join in the echoing brotherhood, reciting the Old Code, accompanied by roaring thunder and driving rain.

Drenched in rain and tears, Bowen covers his head from the forbidding image of King Arthur and the rumble of sound. Breathlessly he recites the Old Code himself, trying to shout down the mad, singsong racket of the spirit voices. "A Knight is sworn to valour...His heart knows only virtue... Blade defends the helpless...Upholds the weak...Speaks only truth..."

Then, realising that his is the only voice, Bowen falls silent. Arthur's voice speaks again."His wrath..."

"...undoes the wicked," continue Arthur and Bowen together.

Then Arthur disappears, in a crash of thunder and a flash of lightning.

Bowen stands alone again, transformed, with rain streaming down his face.

Draco moves out of the darkness and stretches his wings majestically to shield the Knight from the storm.

ONCE AGAIN, KARA tries to raise the villagers to rebellion. Once again One-Eyed Hewe is disdainful. "And we're supposed to follow you and a priest against Einon! To hell more likely!"

"This time we have the Dragon, I tell you," says Kara. "This time we can win."

This brings jeers and laughter from the crowd. "Dragon or no Dragon, we've had enough of your moon-eyed mischief, girl," says Hewe, jabbing Kara in the stomach with his staff. "Get the hell away from here!"

As he raises the staff again, an arrow slices into the ground beside

47

him. It was fired by Bowen who rides up. "Save your strength for the fight against Einon," he says.

"There isn't any fight against Einon," insists Hewe.

"I'm going to start one," says Bowen.

"You and what army?"

Bowen gallops to the top of a hill. "He'll enlist!" he cries, as Draco rises, magnificent and aglow, from behind the horizon...

PREPARATIONS FOR WAR are soon underway. Blacksmiths smelt ploughshares and other implements into molten metal. Newly made weapons hiss as they are dipped in water, before being honed to a lethal sharpness. Women and children work at the making of arrows. Rebels arrive from other villages to swell the ranks.

Gilbert receives an archery lesson, struggling to pull back the bowstring - but when he lets go the bow goes flying and the arrow remains in his hands!

Men are soon exercising with pikes, titling at wooden figures. A command tent is erected, Generals are chosen, parchment maps are studied...

KARA EXERCISES WITH A HEAVY BATTLE-AXE, whirling it above her head. But the momentum sends her staggering backwards into Bowen, who stops her fall. "Easy," he says.

"Oh...thank you."

They are very close. She does not move and he is in no hurry to dislodge her. They remain close as Bowen shows her how to wield the axe properly.

"That could cleave a man's skull," she says.

"Like a pudding," says Bowen reeling back from her spell before flinging the axe which spirals in the air and splits a nearby pumpkin

Bowen shows Kara how to wield an axe

neatly in two.

AT TWILIGHT THE VALLEY IS ALIVE with cooking fires and the laughter and crying of children, alive with the sounds of life.

Bowen and Draco walk the ridge above the camp.

"Einon's fortress is strong," says Bowen.

"Your plan is stronger...Never fear, Einon will fight your battle. But look beyond his petty domain. What can you see?"

Bowen gazes out, transfixed by the beautiful panorama beyond the ridge. "Everything," he says.

"It's yours. Man must make of the world what he can...The day of Dragons is done."

BROK RIDES THROUGH A FIELD, with his favourite falcon perched on his arm. "Hungry, my pet?" he says to the bird, as two beaters flush a covey of doves from the undergrowth. He removes the hood from the falcon's head. "Eat..."

He watches as the falcon soars towards the circling doves...

Brok and his favourite falcon

GILBERT'S ARCHERY SKILLS are improving. He even manages to hit a straw man.

"Don't get all pumped up, Priest," says Hewe. "It's much harder to hit a moving target."

Gilbert takes up the challenge, drawing a bead on a dove winging frantically across the sky. But his arrow misses the dove and strikes the breast of Brok's falcon which plummets to earth and lands at Gilbert's feet. "Look! Look! I got one!" he exclaims.

"You were aiming for the other one."

Suddenly Brok appears on the crest of the ridge, surveying the rebel camp below. Then an echoing roar is heard, as Draco alerts the camp to readiness.

Seeing Bowen riding out and the Dragon perched on a rocky cliff, Brok whips his horse around and rides away.

BROK REPORTS TO THE KING. "...Bowen and the Dragon were in the camp! It's a rebellion I tell you. Hundreds and hundreds of peasants. Only this time they're armed and trained."

"Bowen...and the Dragon is with him...You're sure?" asks Einon, shivering in spite of himself.

ON THE EVE OF BATTLE more and more rebels pour into the camp.

"So many, so fast," says Bowen, strolling through the crowd with Kara. "There's not been enough time. They've not been properly trained."

"The passion and strategy...and hope...you have given them will more than make up for it," she assures him.

"You're very confident."

"You're my confidence. I have never been more sure of anything in my life."

She leads him to his tent where they are met by a delegation of warriors led by Gilbert and One-Eyed Hewe. They present Bowen with a beautiful shield bearing Draco's golden profile as an emblem. "They made it for you," says Kara. "All of them, out of old kettles and ploughs and horseshoes...Gilbert designed it. Hewe hammered and polished it..."

"It was all Kara's idea," says Gilbert.

"A knight's armour should be as bright as his honour," says Kara.

An old woman steps from the crowd and in silent reverence touches Bowen. Others: warriors; women; children; reach out to touch him or give words of thanks. Overcome with emotion, Bowen bolts into his tent.

Kara helps Bowen to put the new armour on. "They expect much," he says.

"They will give much."

The villagers present Bowen with a beautiful shield

"And if I don't lead them to victory?"

"Then you'll have led them farther than they ever dared go before." She steps back to inspect him. "There. All done."

"Not quite," says Bowen. "It is a custom to bestow a favour on a Knight...A veil of scarf that he wears into battle as a token from his lady."

"Do you have a lady?"

"I should be honoured to wear your favour."

"I...I have no such finery. I'm not a lady. I'm a peasant."

"You are the woman I love," says Bowen.

Kara is thrilled but frightened by this blunt confession. "I can give you no favour. I can give nothing. Lost honour can be recovered, not so lost youth. The one thing that was mine to give, Einon stole forever."

"No," says Bowen. "Not your heart."

Kara looks into his eyes, bright with love. Bowen leans down and kisses her.

EINON'S SOLDIERS are readying themselves for battle. Weapons are cached. Food and provisions are stored. Guards prowl the castle battlements.

Einon holds council with his lords. "Peasants fleeing right under your noses - taking grain and livestock with them!"

"But how could we know, your majesty?" says Felton. "A few peasants here and there..."

Brok intervenes, "A few, fop? Hundreds! Armed and spoiling for a fight."

"Then let them have it. One of us is worth a thousand of them," says Felton. "Are you afraid, Sir Brok?"

The snarling Brok almost leaps across the table at Felton, but Einon slams him back. "My brave Felton, an army unto himself," he says,

Dragon slayers

slamming him onto the table. "Fool! I know this man who leads them. And I will not underestimate him or the Dragon."

"Don't fear the Dragon, my son," says Aislinn, silhouetted in the doorway.

"I fear nothing. Nothing!" says Einon.

"Of course not, Einon," says the Queen. "Of course you don't."

Einon pulls his mother aside. "It's just that...sometimes I sense the Dragon. I feel him. As though he were close. But be clear - I don't fear him!"

"There's no need to fear him," say Aislinn, leading Einon into a courtyard where five burly Tartars, all armed to the teeth, await. "A mother's gift to her son. The finest to be had."

"Finest what...?"

"Dragon slayers."

Impulsively, Einon kisses Aislinn's hand.

WITH THE DRACO EMBLEM glittering brightly on his shield, Bowen leads the ragged, proudly determined army out of the camp.

Draco swoops overhead,

51

Kara, Bowen and Gilbert at the head of the ragtag army

Ready for battle!

dipping his wings in salute. Bowen acknowledges the salute with a raised sword and the Dragon banks in the direction of Einon's castle.

A VOLLEY OF FIRE ARROWS bounces harmlessly off the castle wall, and a small troop of shabby, pitiful looking rebels, led by Bowen, are jammed into the road by the castle gates.

From the battlements Einon, Brok and Felton watch the puny force as another pathetic volley of

Draco's surprise!

The King's soldiers ride into a trap

arrows plunks against the stone walls. "Seems you overestimated their numbers, Brok," says Einon, calmly snatching one of the weak arrows out of the air. "And fourteen years hasn't improved their aim very much."

Felton smirks at Brok. "I'm afraid they'll get bored and go home before dark."

"Why wait?" says Einon. "We'll send you out to chase them off, Felton. After all, 'one of us is worth a hundred of them'. The numbers seem about right."

Brok turns, and the blood drains from his face as Draco suddenly appears out of the sunlight, bombarding the battlements with fire balls and sending soldiers flying like toasted marshmallows.

Bowen and Kara in the heat of battle

The Tartar dragon slayers position an unwieldy crossbow on the battlements, loading it with a hideous looking barbed harpoon.

Draco banks and dips behind the castle towers, from where another huge explosion arises, throwing more soldiers into the air. To the cheers of the rebels, the Dragon soars up and over the walls, then banks again for another foray.

Burning scaffolding and falling rock crash all around the dragon slayers as they work their crossbow, but a flaming beam triggers the mechanism and rockets one of them right out of the castle.

Einon realises he's trapped. "We can stay here like sitting ducks or we can crush those rebellious dogs," he snarls.

From her chamber, Aislinn watches the chaos with a look of grim satisfaction on her face.

Four large catapults are loaded with barbed grappling hooks, and are fired off, one after the other. But Draco is a skilled warrior. He dodges them all, catches the last hook and yanks it viciously causing the bolts on one of the catapults to shear off. The machine skews sideways and wedges itself beneath two others. The force of Draco's pull rips up the whole mess, causing more devastation among the dragon slayers and soldiers.

The garrison guards open the castle gates. Einon and his Knights ride out.

"Let's shear them like the sheep they are," calls Einon, spurring his war-horse on. Brok and company ride at his side, while Felton hangs back, troubled at the prospect of the battle ahead.

Einon charges, as Bowen urges the peasant army to retreat into the forest. Soon, all the King's men are wheeling amidst the trees.

Suddenly, rebels carrying torches pop out of the pits where they were concealed. They dip the torches into a trench filled with pitch and fire runs through the forest, creating a barrier which boxes in Einon's men. From the treetops Bowen's archers rain arrows down on the King's force.

Einon realises the error of his rash charge. "Scatter or die!" he yells, as his horse leaps the flames. Others follow his example as his force splits up, only to come face-to-face with more rebel mischief.

Men drop down on them from vines hung in the trees... Arrows fly out of bushes... Logs fall down in front of horses... Other riders fall prey to trip wires, hidden pits and nets. The assault by the peasants is swift and deadly. Einon's men are divided, trapped and overwhelmed.

Backing off surreptitiously, the cowardly Felton bumps into Gilbert. Both men yelp and spin around, their weapons shaking in their hands. Seeing that his opponent is a mere monk, Felton grins brazenly while raising his sword. "Say your prayers, Priest."

Gilbert flinches, as he lets an arrow fly - right into Felton's chest. "God forgive me. That's my prayer."

Einon, his armour ripped open from his left shoulder, whirls his horses around, only to see Bowen almost upon him, sword raised and ready to cleave him in two. As the blade falls, Brok deflects it with a spiked mace, while his horse collides with Bowen. The mace chain wraps itself around the sword. Bowen swings it back and smashes it into Brok's face. Brok sinks down, dead, as Einon escapes.

Gilbert sits shakily on a stump, as a rider sweeps past him.

"Gilbert," cries Kara. "Stop him! It's Einon!"

Hands quivering, Gilbert notches an arrow in his bow, releases it and watches as it strikes Einon.

The King jerks as the arrow pierces his heart. Staggered by the impact, he sucks in his breath. But, although shocked and stunned, he neither falls nor feels the pain...

...DRACO SUDDENLY RECOILS in mid-air, grasping at his chest. As his scales fall back, his breast glows with a crimson throb. He howls in real pain then plummets into the castle below.

KARA, GILBERT AND BOWEN all see Draco's fall.

Startled to be alive, his eyes glinting with understanding, Einon pulls the arrow from his chest. Then a new realisation floods his mind. "The dragon slayers! Nooo!"

He rides fast, towards the castle.

IN THE CASTLE, the three remaining dragon slayers frantically chain Draco to iron spikes driven into the masonry.

Einon charges through the thick wooden gates, just as the dragon slayers swarm in on Draco. "No!" he cries, beating them back with his sword. "I want it alive."

"No..." groans Draco.

"Yes," says Einon, kneeling beside Draco's broken horns. "Safe for all eternity."

ON THE BATTLEFIELD, HEWE and the rebels savour the taste of victory. They stand tall and proud. Men once more.

As Bowen, Kara and Gilbert merge into the forest, Hewe salutes them with upraised sword.

DRACO'S MELANCHOLY TRILL echoes from the castle walls and drifts across the night to the forest's edge where the rebels have set up camp.

"Why does he keep him alive?" asks Bowen. "He must be torturing him."

"No, Einon will not torture him," says Kara. "'Einon will not fall in my lifetime'. Those were Draco's words to me once. I saw him go down. No one touched him. It was when Gilbert shot Einon."

"What are you saying?" says Bowen.

"When my arrow pierced Einon's heart, that was when Draco screamed and fell," says Gilbert.

"Don't you see," says Kara. "Somehow Einon and Draco are connected."

Bowen stares at them, refusing to accept the suggestion...

"Is it true?" asks Kara. "You know it's true."

"No!" says Bowen. "No... Gilbert must have missed. It doesn't matter. Nothing matters except that Draco is still alive."

He turns to the rest of the camp. "I go to save the Dragon. Who goes with me?"

There is no rush to volunteer, just muttered oaths and sullen faces. Bowen turns in disgust to find Kara holding out his sword. "You do not go alone."

Gilbert plops his helmet on his head. "No...not alone..."

Hewe and the others watch in silent shame as the trio march off.

IN A DARK COURTYARD of the castle, Draco lays heavily chained. His feet and tail are shackled tightly to the ground, his head chained down to prevent him from breathing fire on his restraints. With his chin on the cold stone floor, he can only look straight ahead at the wall, or out of the corner of his eye.

He hears footsteps approaching, then a strangled gasp as his guard collapses to the ground, grasping at his throat.

Queen Aislinn steps from the shadows. "Stand where I can see you," says Draco.

"You know why I've come?" says Aislinn, sheathing a bloodstained dagger.

"I know..."

"A sorry end..."

"No," says Draco. "The only end. But I had to wait for a time when mankind would not repeat my sin and let tyranny thrive. When there would be those who remembered the Once-Ways. Remembered that even in the darkness there is still light...I cannot see. Are the stars shining tonight?"

"Brightly, my Lord, brightly," says Aislinn, raising a spear, ready to strike at Draco's heart. "Forgive me."

Suddenly Einon appears and tears the spear from Aislinn's hand. "I know why you brought me the dragon slayers, Mother. You wanted them to kill him. You wanted me dead."

"I wanted to correct a mistake made fourteen years ago," she replies. "When I saved a creature not worth saving."

"How unmotherly of you," says Einon in a voice like ice.

Aislinn does not flinch as he forces her back into the shadows, his murderous intentions all too clear to Draco.

"No-o-o-o!" cries the Dragon...

Aislinn raises a spear to kill Draco

KARA LEADS BOWEN AND GILBERT through the castle's secret passages. Bowen charges for the courtyard door.

"Not that way," warns Kara. "The guards are everywhere."

"Then that's our way," says a voice from the darkness. The trio turn to see One-Eyed Hewe with a small band of rebels. "We've got to open the gates for the rest of us waiting outside."

Touched by this show of loyalty, Bowen claps Hewe on the shoulder.

"Go save your Dragon, Sir Bowen," says Hewe, opening a door to the castle grounds and motioning his men through it.

Kara points to the other stairway. "This leads to Einon's quarters."

FROM THE SECRET PASSAGE, Bowen, Kara and Gilbert creep into Einon's bedchamber and the King is sprawled on his bed.

"What a pleasant surprise," he says. "I expected you, Knight. But with my bride-to-be, as well? And a Priest to wed us."

"To bury you Einon," says Bowen, charging at the bed but stabbing only bedclothes as Einon whirls away.

"Well, to bury one of us," says the King, his blade meeting Bowen's.

The two engage in fast and furious swordplay which takes them out onto a stairwell. "We know each other's every move," says Einon. "But I'm younger and faster."

"I'll slow you," says Bowen, "so you won't get any older."

As the sword fight continues, Hewe and his marauders descend on the castle guards, slaying them and opening the gates, only to find an outer gate beyond, this is also guarded. But before Hewe and his men can advance further, a sentry blows a ram's horn alarm.

Bowen grins, as his blade flashes furiously at Einon. "My rebels are storming your castle."

"Pity you won't live to see them fail," says Einon, almost slicing off the Knight's ear.

This angers Bowen, who launches a wild sally which Einon coolly deflects. "Practise what you preach, mentor. Purpose, not passion, remember?"

Bowen intensifies his reckless assault.

"Nerve cold-blue..." chides Einon, "...Blade blood-red."

"I still have one more lesson to teach you," says Bowen.

"And what, pray, is that?"

"The last one your father learned."

Einon laughs and charges again. Blades lock and, with renewed vigour, Bowen manoeuvres Einon around and back up the stairs.

Hewe and his troop struggle with Einon's soldiers and manage to prise the outer gates open, allowing their compatriots to pour into the castle, with wild war cries.

BOWEN AND EINON have fought their way into the half-crumbled, roofless tower. They duel over and around building materials and scaffolding, sparks flying from their clanging blades.

Bowen's blade cracks against masonry. Einon whirls in without mercy, as Bowen tosses the broken hilt at him before diving into a clutter of scaffolding. Splinters fly as Einon chops and hacks away, trying to finish the Knight once and for all. He laughs in malicious glee, his eyes glinting like a madman. "Fool! You lost before you began. I am immortal!"

Bowen leaps up, twirling onto a cross beam, out and over Einon, who spins to cut him down before he lands.

Kara throws her axe to Bowen. He catches it and turns on Einon who is jarred back. Bowen sends the axe flying through the air. It just misses the King's head before burying itself in the wooden shutter of a window. Einon strikes back. Bowen leaps his thrust and jumps onto a low sill to yank the axe free. But it won't budge.

Einon snarls and lunges. Bowen pushes off from the sill and, clinging to the axe handle, rides the shutter as it swings outwards. Einon's momentum carries him out of the window and tumbles him into space.

The King's body falls through scaffolding, careens into the cistern in a cacophony of clatter, clutter and dust and plunges into the water.

Kara and Gilbert dash to the window, as Bowen clings to the axe handle on the swinging shutter. All three look down. Einon has disappeared. "So much for his immortality," says Bowen.

But then, from the courtyard below, comes the Dragon's agonised scream.

"Draco!" cries Bowen, as the axe dislodges itself and sends him tumbling into space. He grabs a pulley line attached to the tower and spirals down into the courtyard, arriving just in time to prevent one of the dragon slayers from killing Draco.

Another dragon slayer aims a fire-arrow at Bowen from the battlements, but before he can unleash the arrow, Draco's nostril shoots a fireball which ricochets off the cobbles and engulfs the dragon slayer, sending him plummeting off the castle wall.

USING THE DRAGON SLAYER'S oversized axe, Bowen hacks at Draco's shackles.

"You should have let them do it," says Draco. "Now you must."

"What?" asks Bowen.

"Even as the heart binds Einon to me in life, it binds us in death."

"That's not true."

"You've seen that it is," says Draco. "Through the heart we share each other's pains and power. But in my heart beats the Life Source. For Einon to die, I must die."

Kara arrives, having made her way down from the tower. "Einon is dead," says Bowen. "Tell him, Kara."

But Kara is uncertain. She knows what she has seen. She also knows Draco. "I...I...don't know..."

"You saw it," says Bowen.

"He lives," insists Draco.

"It doesn't matter," says Bowen, desperately. "Our rebels have stormed the castle. Alive or dead, Einon's beaten. We've won!"

"You will never win until Einon's evil is destroyed," says Draco. "And to do that, you must destroy me."

"No!" says Bowen.

"Once you swore your sword and service were mine. To call when I had need of you. I hold you to your vow, Knight...He's coming! Coming to stop you...Strike before it's too late."

"You are the last..."

"My time is over. Strike!" says Draco.

"You're my friend."

"Then, as my friend, strike!"

"I can't."

"Then I will make you," says Draco, roaring and lunging at Bowen, with his snapping fangs.

Bowen evades the blow, but Draco lashes out again, trying to provoke him. Again the Knight dodges the sharp teeth.

"Fight back," says Draco, rattling his chains and shooting out a jet of flame at Bowen.

Kara screams, but Bowen holds his ground as the flame misses him by inches.

"Defend yourself," says Draco.

But Bowen flings the axe to the ground.

"Pick it up!" cries Draco.

Kara stoops for the axe, but Einon's blade is suddenly at her throat. He is battered and bloody, but very much alive.

Draco wails in misery, as Bowen moves for the axe.

"Move and she dies," says Einon.

Gilbert arrives and freezes, watching helplessly. It's stalemate, until Draco viciously sinks his fangs into his own claw - and it is Einon who feels the pain in his sword hand. The sword clatters to the ground.

Instantly realising what he must do, Bowen picks up the axe, as Kara breaks from Einon.

Einon draws his dagger and, sure of his immortality, charges Bowen.

Bowen sets to meet him, but looks back at Draco who is exposing his chest for the blow, his scales falling back revealing the scar.

But Einon keeps coming, with murder in his eyes. "Only expose your back to a corpse," he says to Bowen.

Bowen raises the axe to meet him, but in a blur he wheels and hurls the axe the other way - at Draco.

The axe twirls in the air and buries itself in Draco's scarred breast. The Dragon folds with the impact.

Einon is jerked by the force that Draco feels, but his momentum carries him right into Bowen who, in one powerful movement, stabs Einon with his own dagger and heaves him over his head.

The dead King crashes down, beside Draco.

"You are a corpse..." says Bowen, as Einon gives a last, strangled gasp before closing his eyes.

BOWEN WATCHES DRACO SMILE as his eyelids flutter down.

Hewe and the other rebels arrive to see the Knight kneeling forlornly over his friend's still body.

"What now, Dragon?" asks Bowen. "You abandon us now that we're free. Without you, what do we do? Where do we turn...?"

At that moment, Draco's physical presence dissolves into a translucent iridescence, its light hovering in front of Bowen. "...To the stars, Bowen. To the stars," whispers Draco's voice.

Everyone present has heard it. None will ever forget it.

They watch as the ethereal glow rises up and floats above the rebels, above the castle walls and out into the night. The light of Draco's fiery soul accelerates above the mountains, increasing into a brilliant density, before streaking towards the heavens like a ruby comet. Then, echoing above the earth comes the sound of Draco's song, sweet, clear and joyous.

Bowen gazes heavenwards, a strange knowledge in his eyes, a perception of peace and transformation. Gilbert and Kara share his wonder.

In the sky the stars suddenly dim and fade as the strange light shoots across night's black curtain toward the constellation Draco where, for just an instant, it erupts into a blazing profile of Draco then fades away along with Draco's song.

The other stars return to the heavens as Kara embraces Bowen and Gilbert crosses himself.

THE NEW STAR glitters brilliantly, more vivid, more lustrous than the others. Its gleaming rays beam down upon Bowen, Kara and Gilbert, their upturned faces bathed in its exquisite light.

DragonHeart
THE END